MICROCOSM · PUBLISHING

Microcosm Publishing is Portland's most diversified publishing house and distributor with a focus on the colorful, authentic, and empowering. Our books and zines have put your power in your hands since 1996, equipping readers to make positive changes in their lives and in the world around them. Microcosm emphasizes skill-building, showing hidden histories, and fostering creativity through challenging conventional publishing wisdom with books and bookettes about DIY skills, food, bicycling, gender, self-care, and social justice. What was once a distro and record label was started by Joe Biel in his bedroom and has become among the oldest independent publishing houses in Portland, OR. We are a politically moderate, centrist publisher in a world that has inched to the right for the past 80 years.

INTRODUCTION

Otter Lieffe

s a trans woman and an ecologist, I find queerness in non-human nature to be a profoundly important subject. There's something about knowing that there are lesbian lizards in the world and orgies of gay manatees, polyamorous oystercatchers and trans clownfish, bisexual red deer and masturbating baboons and kissing zebras that just gives me hope. I have been writing on the subject for years in my novels, *Margins and Murmurations* and *Conserve and Control* and on my blog, sharing the knowledge that our beautiful community extends far beyond the realms of human culture.

As so many young nature-lovers, I grew up with David Attenborough's wildlife programs and I never once heard about these things. It was all 'male meets female, seduces her with his bright feathers or funky dance and they very quickly mate.' The implication has always been that that the whole point of life is to make little baby animals and there was nothing in the great natural world that might challenge the cis-het norms of biologists.

I'm so glad that wasn't all there was to learn.

QUEER PLANET

Few words have been as redefined and debated over as "queer." I have a lot of strong feelings about this word, political, social, personal. In this zine, I've decided to play fast and loose, defining queer as anything outside of those cis-het (and monosexual and monogamous and "vanilla" and non-intersex) norms that biologists and wildlife documentaries have taught us to expect. So gay penguins are definitely queer, and also polyandrogynous oystercatchers. Intersex grizzly bears, kinky dolphins, and also sex-changing parrotfish.

Although I'm aware of the dangers of talking about "kinky dolphins" or "lesbian lizards," I also believe that in this disconnected, alienated world, we probably don't anthropomorphize other species nearly enough.

Also as a central character from my novel *Margins and Murmurations* mentions:

> There's an interesting double-bind. If animals are totally straight and cis and never queer—which is what scientists always assume—then being queer is "unnatural" and "artificial." If animals are sometimes queer and humans are sometimes queer, then human queers are "beasts, no better than animals." Either way we lose.

The point of highlighting queerness in non-human nature then is not to justify our existence as trans and queer people with examples from biology (although if you need to shut down someone who claims queerness is "unnatural," then this zine could definitely come in useful).

This project is in fact to show that our beautiful queer community, human and non-human, is something to celebrate.

The format of a coloring zine—and book—makes this information accessible to a wider range of people who might not pick up obscure ecology journals. The beautiful illustrations of diverse animals—drawn by talented artist, Anja Van Geert—bring the subject to life. We hope you share in this celebration coloring in your favourite pictures alone and with loved ones. After all, at the end of the day, queerness is all about community.

CASSOWARY (*Casuarius spp.*)

Found: In the tropical forests of New Guinea (Papua New Guinea and Indonesia), East Nusa Tenggara, the Maluku Islands, and northeastern Australia.

Height: up to 2 m

Weight: up to 58.6 kg

Conservation status: The southern cassowary is endangered in Queensland

Cassowaries are surely one of the most magnificent birds on earth. Flightless and massive with a brightly-colored helmet used for crashing through forests, they also have a unique genital anatomy.

Most male birds in the world don't have a penis, but Cassowary males do. As it's involved in sex but isn't connected to internal organs, scientists sometimes call it a male clitoris. All females also possess a phallus which is basically the same, just a little smaller. On top of that, like other birds they mate and lay eggs through another orifice called the cloaca which, by the way, is also their anus.

Magnificent and pretty special.

GRIZZLY BEARS (*Ursus arctos horribilis*)

Found: Coastal North America

Length: up to 198 cm

Weight: up to 360 kg

Conservation status: Least concern

Grizzlies are maybe a surprising addition to a book on queer animals, but they shouldn't be. Powerful, fierce, they are also sometimes gay and intersex. Females often bond for a few seasons raising cubs and defending food—even heading out into the cold and visiting each other during hibernation. One study showed up to 20% of females engaging in these companionships at some point in their life; sometimes involving three, four or even five female bears.

Some populations of grizzlies have a higher-than average proportion of intersex members - up to 25 percent in some areas. For grizzlies that means having genetics and internal reproductive organs associated with females, combined with a "penis-like organ". Most intersex grizzlies are parents and some give birth through the tip of their penis.

Now you know.

MUTE SWANS (*Cygnus olor*)

Found: Native to Eurosiberia and North Africa. Introduced to North America, Australasia and South Africa

Length: up to 170 cm

Weight: up to 23 kg

Conservation status: Least concern

For many, swans are the epitome of respectable, and straight, monogamy. We all know that they mate together for life and create ideal families.

That's not entirely accurate.

Mute swans are actually known to happily go off and create gay partnerships, both male and female, sometimes building nests and raising chicks together. Many are exclusively into same-sex hook ups, and non-breeding birds will gather into their own flocks seperate from the breeders.

But at least they're faithful, right? Nope. Some mate with other birds while still paired with their partner and some of these "flings" involve females mounting males. They don't even limit themselves to fun within their species and will get together with other kinds of swans and even geese. In the closely related Black swan, 14% of all bonds involve two males pairing with a female.

Maybe swans *do* represent family values for some, but they're probably not the values many would have expected.

LONG-EARED HEDGEHOGS (*Hemiechinus auritus*)

Found: Steppes and desert of Central Asia and the Middle East.

Length: up to 27cm

Weight: up to 400 grams

Conservation status: Least concern

Long-eared hedgehogs aren't super famous in the queer animal world. They're no giraffe, koala or dolphin. But they are incredibly cute. And super into oral sex.

A typical "lesbian interaction" according to the research begins at dusk. It starts with some cuddling and mutual rubbing and quickly escalates to sniffing, licking and nibbling each other's genitals. Sometimes a female will lift her butt in the air to give her partner better access. Sometimes they both do it to initiate mounting.

Heterosexual pairs are into it as well, but just to be clear, it's the male that sniffs and licks the female.

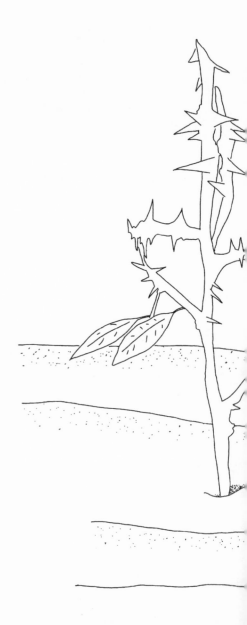

PARROTFISH (Several Species, family: Scaridae/Scarinae)

Found: in coral reefs, rocky coasts, and seagrass beds particularly in the Indo-Pacific

Size: Some species reach up to 1.3 metres in length

Conservation status: Varied, depends on species

Parrotfish must be one of the most beautifully patterned and multi-colored fish in the sea. They're also sex-changing, multi-gendered, wonderfully complex beauties. Scientists call them "sequential hermaphrodites" as, along with 25% of coral reef fish species, parrotfish fully change sex, sometimes repeatedly during their lifetimes.

As for gender, striped parrotfish (*Scarus croicensis*) have such complex lives, they've been assigned five distinct genders based on if they've changed sex or not, the kind of genitals they currently have (biologists love that kind of thing) and their color. With multiple sexes and genders within one lifetime and plenty of fluidity between them, parrotfishes are as queer as they come. So much so that scientists needed a word for those unusual species who *don't* change sex, those with distinct sexes in which males remain males and females remain female. It's gonochoristic, by the way. You're welcome.

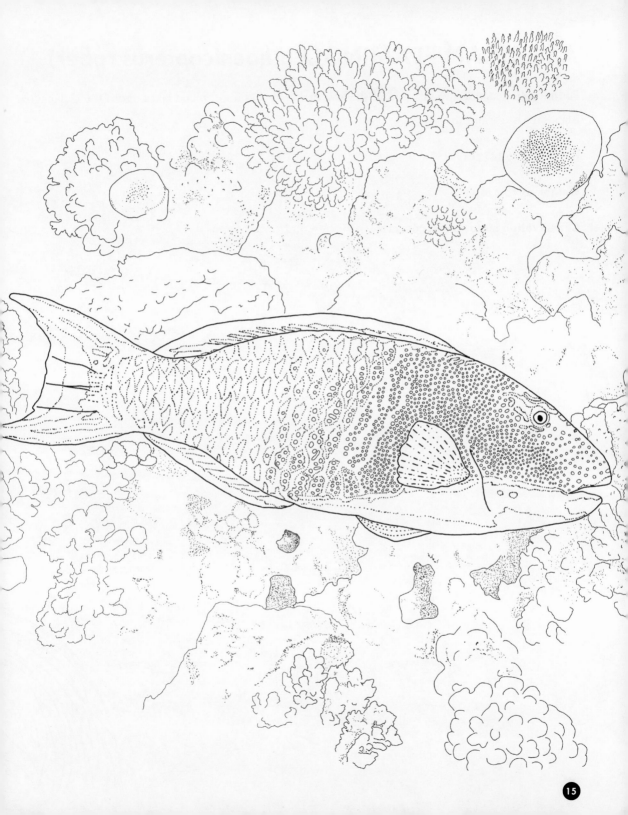

AMERICAN FLAMINGO (*Phoenicopterus ruber*)

Found: saline lagoons, mudflats, and shallow, brackish coastal or inland lakes. From the Galápagos islands to the caribbean

Height: up to 145 cm

Weight: up to 2.8kg

Conservation status: Least concern

Elegant, glamorous and outrageously pink, no-one should be too surprised that flamingos can be queer. Both males and females form same-sex pairs, feeding, travelling and sleeping with their partners. Female pairs apparently engage in "full genital contact" and male pairs build super sized nests to incubate, hatch and raise foster chicks. Sometimes they have no previous experience with different-sex partners and sometimes they're bi. One thing's for certain though, they are always fabulous.

BATS (order: Chiroptera)

Species: over 1,200 individual species, around 20% of all mammal species

Found: Throughout the world, with the exception of extremely cold regions

Size: The largest species of bat can weigh up to 1.6 kg and have a wingspan of 1.7 m

Conservation status: Varied, depends on species

Bats might not be everyone's favourite animal, but they have intimate, sexual lives and more than twenty species have been observed "engaging in homosexual behaviour"—from mutual grooming to cross-species gay sex.

Grey-headed flying foxes ((*Pteropus poliocephalus*) of all sexes get into nibbling the chests and wings of their same-sex partners. Vampire bats (subfamily: Desmodontinae) perform fellatio on each other. Male Indian flying foxes (*Pteropus medius)* mount each other with erections while play-wrestling. Even Natterer's (*Myotis nattereri*) and Daubenton's (*Myotis daubentonii)*) bats, two totally different species have been seen having gay fun together.

There are definitely some queer vampire stories to be told there.

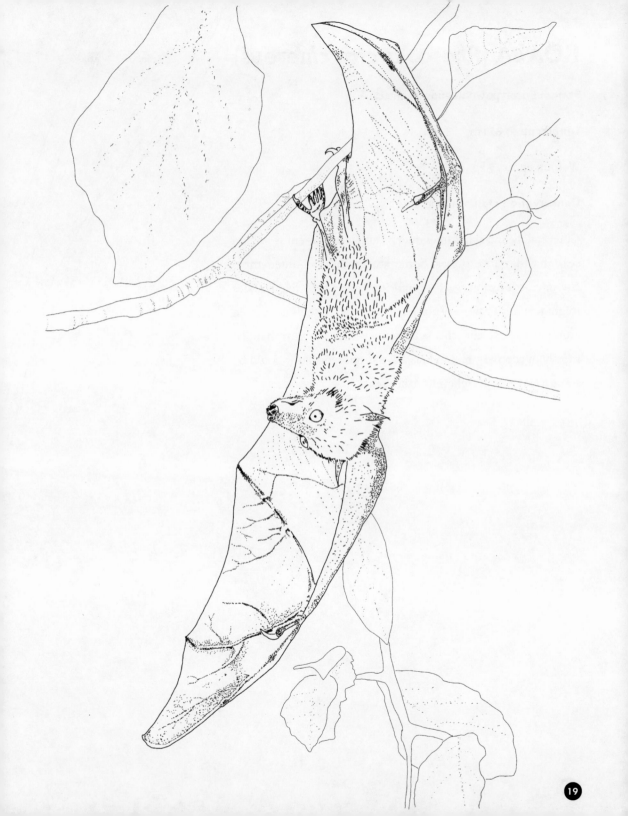

KOALA (*Phascolarctos cinereus*)

Found: Eucalypt woodlands in Australia

Length: up to 85 cm

Weight: up to 15 kg

Conservation status: Vulnerable

Cute, cuddly and sometimes queer. Female koalas enjoy lesbian sex, and they love orgies. Some studies have counted three gay interactions for every straight one and up to five females might join in to have *very* noisy sex together. In their continued attempts to "explain" this behaviour, which seems to happen mostly in captivity, researchers have proposed that it could be some kind of stress reliever. Makes sense.

FERAL PIGEON (*Columba livia domestica*)

Found: Towns and cities everywhere!

Length: up to 37 cm

Weight: up to 380g

Conservation status: Least concern

Few birds are as familiar to city-dwellers around the world as the feral pigeon. Some love them, some hate them, but they are pretty much everywhere. You guessed it: they're queer. Both males and females create same-sex pairs, building nests together and having sex. If a male partner deserts a brood or dies, hens will sometimes pair up, lay eggs and incubate them.

Next time you see a flock of pigeons in a city square, just remember, humans aren't the only queers in the city.

WHIPTAIL LIZARD (*Cnemidophorus spp.,*
Aspidoscelis spp.)

Found: Mostly deserts in Southwestern United States, South and Central America, and the West Indies.

Size: varies

Conservation status: varies

Rarely mentioned and often ignored as an anomaly or an evolutionary dead end (and haven't we all heard that before?), there are several species of lizard, at least eight in the south-west of North America, who are completely female. There is not a single male in these species and there is no need for reproductive sex: females produce fertile eggs all by themselves.

As we all know—because we've been told this lie since birth—animals only have sex to make little baby animals, so for a long time, scientists assumed these female-only lizards didn't, wouldn't, or couldn't have sex. After all, what would be the point?

They do. A lot. In fact, they follow a highly intricate courtship pattern and two females sharing a burrow and sleeping there together will cycle their hormones, one with high progesterone levels who becomes the top, and one with high estradiol levels who becomes the bottom. After a few weeks, they switch hormone levels and position.

Major scientific journals still refer to the whiptail lizards as "celibate" despite all the—great deal of—lesbian sex going on right in front of the biologists' homophobic eyes. Presumably, for some commentators at least, unless there's a male penetrating a female, there simply is no sex.

Interesting fact: studies have shown that compared with similar species that have both males and females, the female-only whiptail species are four times less aggressive and have a much less marked dominance hierarchy. Surprised? Didn't think so.

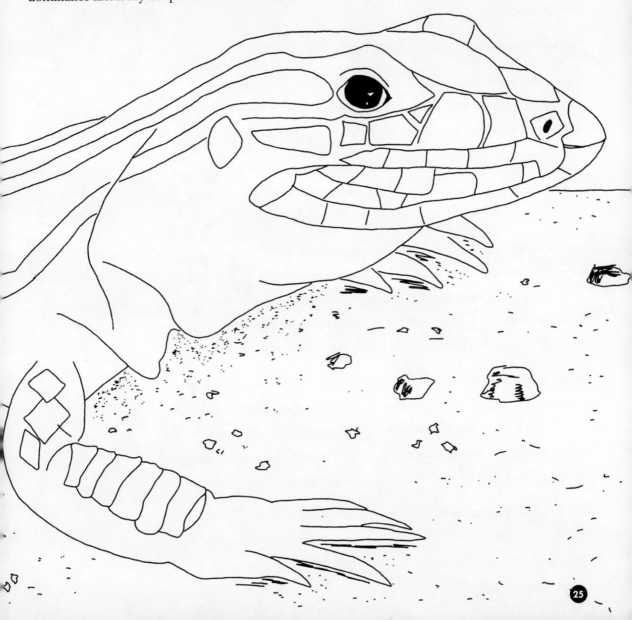

CLOWNFISH (subfamily: Amphiprioninae)

Found: shallow waters and reefs. Indian sea, including the Red Sea. Pacific Oceans, including the Great Barrier Reef, Southeast Asia, Japan, and the Indo-Malaysian region.

Length: up to 17 cm

Conservation status: Varies

The more I learn about queerness in nature, the happier it makes me. Clownfish, for example, change sex several times during their lifetime. Because yes everyone, Nemo was totally trans.

Orange Clownfish (*Amphiprion percula*), those famous little fish living among the poisonous tentacles of sea anemones can change twice—from asexual juveniles to male and from male to female.

For them, size confers dominance. Bigger is better. And as females are bigger than males, they're also more dominant. A single female and male form a cozy monogamous straight relationship (don't worry, it won't last forever) and live together in their poisonous anemone along with some differently sized asexual juveniles who float in on the current.

If the female dies or leaves (or like in the movie, gets eaten by a big barracuda), the male starts to buff up, put on weight and changes sex to female. That same fish then becomes the new female of the anemone and one of the juveniles sexually matures and becomes a male to take her place. And back we go to cozy monogamous straightness…

So, you know, in the realistic version of the movie, Nemo's mom got eaten, Nemo's dad became his new mom and agender Nemo transitioned to male and married her. Really, I can't imagine why they changed it.

DOLPHINS (infraorder Cetacea, 40 species)

Found: Widespread, mostly warmer waters of tropical zones

Size: Common bottlenose dolphins can measure up to 3.5 m and weigh up to 500 kg

Conservation status: Varies

Dolphins are one of the most charismatic groups of animals in the world. From Flipper to Seaworld, they are adored by humans everywhere (except when being hunted, poisoned and incarcerated, obviously.) Little did we know that they're also total perverts.

Bottlenose dolphins (*Tursiops spp.*) are big into oral sex. Males and females alike will insert their snout into the genital slit of another, stimulating their partner and pushing them along in the water, just for fun. Scientists call it "beak-genital propulsion" by the way, which is pretty romantic. Males and females both enjoy other kinds of penetration too, sometimes from another dolphin's fin or tail.

Atlantic Spotted Dolphins (*Stenella frontalis*) have a particularly fun way to please each other, known as a "genital buzz." One dolphin can direct a sexy sound wave through the water, stimulating their partner. They're also sexually pursued by Bottlenoses—a totally different species—sometimes mating with two bottlenoses at the same time. Sometimes these pursuits are playful, sometimes aggressive. Scientists believe that these sexual pursuits may lead to cooperation on hunts.

They get even more creative than that. Male Botos (*Inia geoffrensis*) have been seen penetrating their male partner's blowhole—in the top of his head. That's pretty kinky.

Talkative, funny, beautiful—dolphins are many things. But vanilla certainly isn't one of them.

WEST INDIAN MANATEES (*Trichechus manatus*)

Found: Coastal waters and rivers of southeastern US, the Caribbean and northeastern Brazil

Length: up to 3.5 m

Weight: up to 600 kg

Conservation status: Vulnerable

These manatees are large aquatic mammals that live in the Caribbean, northeastern Brazil and the southeast of North America. Despite common assumptions about queerness in the animal kingdom, these beautiful mammals are really very gay. Male manatees of all ages commonly engage in gay sex.

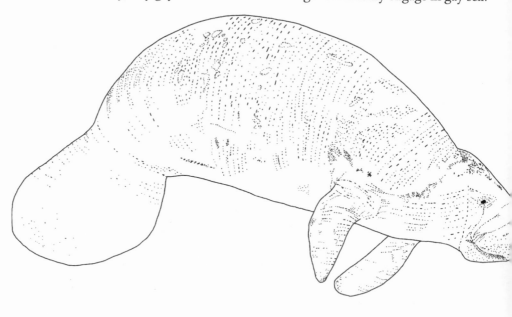

And it's a total party.

Two male manatees will sometimes begin sex by kissing their muzzles together above the water. They sometimes mate in a head to tail position, nibble each other's bits and masturbate each other with a flipper. All this is quite different to straight sex in this species and *generally lasts two to four times as long.*

Often males form orgies of up to four, kissing, thrusting and rubbing their dicks against each other. They have also been known to make uniquely gay sounds of pleasure, different again to the sounds made during straight coupling. You know . . . *gay-er.*

Manatees were long mistaken for mermaids and sirens—those feminine, boundary-crossing creatures who seduced sailors with their beauty and hypnotising songs. Their closest living relatives, incidentally, are hyraxes and elephants. Who could have guessed?

But beauty and mystery won't be enough to save this beautiful species. The West Indian manatees are endangered by hunting, pollution and collisions with boats and are down to 10,000 individuals in the wild. Tragically, without immediate action, they, and their raunchy sex lives, may very well soon go extinct.

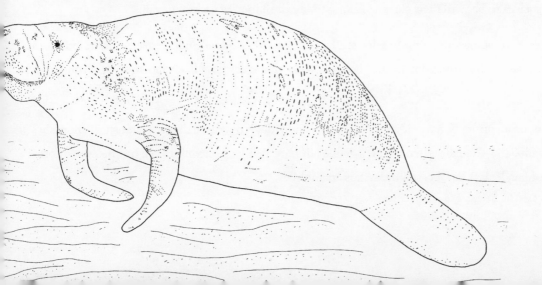

RED DEER (*Cervus elaphus*)

Found: Most of Europe, parts of western Asia, and central Asia. Parts of northwestern Africa. Introduced to South America and Australia

Length: up to 250 cm

Weight: up to 240 kg

Conservation status: Least concern

Because yes, does can be lesbian, bi and they can be tops too.

Red deer are common across North Africa, Europe and Southwest Asia. They have a breeding season, aka "ruts," for about a month each year and during the rest of their time, mature adults live mostly in single sex groups. It's then, when they're not focused on breeding, that the does have a whole lot of gay sex.

It's pretty much the norm and about 70% of all does mate with each other outside the rut. Around a third play exclusively with other does and the rest are bi. They are divided more or less equally into tops ("mounters"), bottoms ("mountees") and versatiles. Occasionally when stags and does come together, it's the doe who tops the stag.

Both does and stags form pair bonds with members of their own sex and does in particular will travel great distances to be with their partner, calling to her until they're together again.

They also have some other fun gender stuff going on. Most females don't have antlers but some do. Most stags do but some don't. And the stags without antlers have been shown to be stronger and fitter.

Scientists, unsurprisingly, have either ignored these individuals or erased them as "statistical anomalies" (sound familiar?). Actually, of course, it's gender fluidity, gender nonconformity, maybe even another couple of genders. What it certainly isn't, is an anomaly.

Speaking of antlers...for red deer they are an erogenous zone and stags have been observed masturbating by rubbing their antlers against vegetation, sometimes getting hard and ejaculating in the process. Now you know.

EURASIAN OYSTERCATCHER (*Haematopus ostralegus*)

Found: Western Europe, central Eurosiberia, Kamchatka, China, and the western coast of Korea.

Length: up to 45 cm

Conservation status: Near threatened

Oystercatchers are common shore birds across Europe. They often live in flocks and although most oystercatchers form monogamous pair bonds for breeding (you know, that story . . .), others have a very fun sex life.

Occasionally they get into a bisexual ménage à trois—two males with a female, or two females with a male—in which they all have an intimate relationship with each other. Females affectionately preen each other, males give each other courtship displays and all three have sex. These trios can last up to twelve years, aren't always exclusive, and members engage in hetero promiscuity outside the trio.

About 30% of oystercatcher populations are non-breeding, but just the same, they engage in sexual behaviour within and without their bonded pairs and trios. Females sometimes top males and it has been estimated that a straight pair will have sex 700 times during the breeding season. 700 times for one single clutch of eggs. For oystercatchers at least, sex is about much more than just breeding.

GIRAFFES (*Giraffa camelopardalis*)

Found: Savannas and woodlands. Range from Chad in the north to South Africa in the south, and from Niger in the west to Somalia in the east.

Height: Up to 5.88 m tall

Weight: up to 1,192 kg

Conservation status: Vulnerable

Few animals have filled as many children's picture books as the mighty giraffe. Little do those illustrators know how very gay they are.

Male giraffes have a unique form of flirting, and seduction, called necking. For up to an hour they'll stand next to each other, usually facing in opposite directions and gently rub their necks all over each other's bodies leading to erections all round and often orgasms. They might get excited enough to mount each other too, sometimes repeatedly and sometimes in groups of up to four or five. That's a lot of neck.

Giraffes are not big breeders—in fact only a small percentage of adults breed at all. In one study, during 3,200 hours of detailed study over an entire year, only one single straight mating was observed. In another study on the other hand, gay mounting and necking made up an impressive 94% of all giraffe sexual activity.

So next time you see a giraffe in a picture book or a commercial or on the cover of a magazine, just remember: super gay.

BONOBO (*Pan paniscus*)

Found: Primary and secondary forests in the Congo Basin.

Height: up to 115 cm

Weight: up to 60kg

Conservation status: Endangered

If there is one species which stands alone as practically a queer superstar of the primate world it's the bonobo. This species, *Pan paniscus*—our closest living relative along with the chimpanzee—is endangered and lives only in a single area of the DRC. They have, as you may have heard, an incredibly raunchy sex life.

Almost all bonobos are bi and more than two thirds of female sex is with other females. Every couple of hours, a female engages in the wonderfully euphemistic "GG (genital-genital) rubbing" with other females.

The guys also get up to their fair share of gay fun. One of their favourite positions—known by the infinitely creative scientific community as "penis-fencing"—involves both partners hanging from a branch facing each other, swinging their hips and rubbing dicks. They also suck, and kiss with a lot of tongue. Males and females masturbate too, and males use inanimate objects for that purpose. And there are orgies. And from time to time they hook up with redtail monkeys (*Cercopithecus ascanius*)—a totally different species.

Sex is a defining point of bonobo life and is crucial for reconciliation and sharing, integrating new arrivals, forming coalitions and trade. They've even developed a set of hand signals to communicate what kind of fun they're up for including 25 gestures from "come over here and let's get it on" to "turn around" and "open your legs"—Grindr and OkCupid eat your heart out.

Most of these gestures are symbolic, but some are more abstract and some scientists think they represent the beginnings of complex language. The more sexual diversity, the more a species needs to communicate their desires. Enough said.

CHINSTRAP PENGUIN (*Pygoscelis antarcticus*)

Found: islands and shores in the Southern Pacific and the Antarctic Oceans

Height: up to 76 cm

Weight: up to 5.3 kg

Conservation status: Least concern

Everyone loves penguins, but not everyone loves gay penguins.

Since at least 1911, penguins have been observed "engaging in homosexual behaviour." What's interesting is that the earliest report was considered too shocking, the behaviour too depraved, to be made public. Private copies of the report were *translated into Greek* to keep them secret.

But the news got out. In the late 1990's, in a New York zoo, two male chinstrap penguins raised a chick. Roy and Silo became penguin superstars and their story was told in a play and at least two children's books. To this day, this small penguin family is being used as an argument by both North American liberals and the Christian right. Who knew that penguins could be so controversial?

ABOUT THE AUTHORS

Otter Lieffe

Otter Lieffe is a working class, femme, trans woman and the author of three trans feminist novels—*Margins and Murmurations, Conserve and Control* and *Dignity*. Most recently, her short story *Synergy* was published in *Our Entangled Future,* an anthology on social change and the climate crisis. She holds a degree in Ecology and Conservation and has been in love with the living beings around her since a very young age.

A grassroots community organiser for over two decades, Otter has worked and organised in Europe, the Middle-East and Latin America with a particular focus on the intersection of gender, queerness and environmental struggles. Since publishing her first novel in 2017, Otter has been building networks to counter the systemic oppressions faced by working-class trans women. In 2019, she launched her new organisation, Trans Feminism International (transfeminism.net), organising to meet the material needs of trans women. You can find her online at otterlieffe.com

Anja Van Geert

After completing a PhD in Plant Ecology, Anja Van Geert has been part of many ecological projects and adventures including growing herbs at an urban farm in her home town of Brussels. She currently lives in Brighton, UK organising queer tea ceremonies and herb meditations. She is a breathwork facilitator by trade and is starting out on a new artistic journey. Anja drew the images for this zine, curled up with her cat Moisey, with *Buffy the Vampire Slayer* in the background. You can find her at pinprimrose.co.uk